Kitty secrets

QEB

Camilla de la Bédoyère

Quarto is the authority on a wide range of topics.
Quarto educates, entertains and enriches the lives of
our readers—enthusiasts and lovers of hands-on living.
www.quartoknows.com

© 2017 Quarto Publishing plc

First published in 2017 by QEB Publishing,
an imprint of The Quarto Group
6 Orchard Road, Suite 100
Lake Forest, CA 92630
T: +1 949 380 7510
F: +1 949 380 7575
www.QuartoKnows.com

A CIP record for this book is
available from the Library of Congress.

ISBN: 978 1 68297 367 7

Manufactured in Shenzhen, China RD112017

9 8 7 6 5 4 3 2 1

FSC
www.fsc.org
MIX
Paper from
responsible sources
FSC® C101537

A KITTY PROFILE on each breed
contains information about **size,
color, eye color,** and **energy level.**

KITTY PROFILE

 Large

 Usually copper-brown
with some black

 Green, copper, gold

 ★★★★

CONTENTS

# ABYSSINIAN

KITTY PROFILE

🐾🐾·· Medium

⬛⬛⬛⬜ Various, but usually red-brown

👁👁 Amber, green, hazel

★★★★

Cat-lovers adore Abyssinians because they are a perfect blend of beauty and brains. Their glossy fur almost glows in the sunlight and they love to play outdoors, exploring every tree and corner of the garden. Even little kittens love to jump and climb!

SHHH, TOP SECRET!

I like to be helpful. I'm very good at walking across keyboards and sitting on books!

AMERICAN BOBTAIL

KITTY PROFILE

Medium

Any

Any

★★★★★

When one of these short-tailed kitties is ready to play, it will bring its toys to you and drop them at your feet! American Bobtails look wild, with their spots and stripes, but they will quickly win your hearts with their friendly faces and sweet natures.

SHHH, TOP SECRET!

We are quiet kittens, but we chirp and trill to say we love you!

AMERICAN CURL

KITTY PROFILE

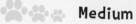 Medium

▪▪▪▪□ Any

👁 👁 Any

🐈 ★★★★

When a cat wants your attention it meows or rubs its cheeks against your legs. An American Curl likes lots of attention, so don't be surprised if these cute kitties gently pat your face with their paws, lick your nose, or jump onto your bed to wake you up!

SHHH, TOP SECRET!

We are born with straight ears, but they curl when we are about ten days old!

AMERICAN SHORTHAIR

KITTY PROFILE

 Medium to large

 Any

 Any

 ★★★

Everyone knows that cats like the lazy life! American Shorthairs are special cats because they prefer to work hard and are always busy outdoors looking for mice or bugs to chase. These kittens will grow up to be sturdy, strong, and loyal members of the family.

SHHH, TOP SECRET!

We're very popular with farmers and we love to be around other animals.

AMERICAN WIREHAIR

KITTY PROFILE

🐾🐾🐾 Medium to large

▣▣▣▢ Any

👁👁 Any but usually gold

🐈 ★★★

If you run your hand over the coat of an American Wirehair you can feel the hairs are frizzy, not smooth. Even these kittens' whiskers are curly! Wirehair cats are a type of American Shorthair, and they share the same friendly, playful nature.

SHHH, TOP SECRET!

Almost anything makes us happy enough to start purring loudly!

BALINESE

KITTY PROFILE

 Medium

 Ivory, cream

  Sapphire blue

★★★★

These gorgeous kittens have the slender, elegant bodies of Siamese cats, but they have long hair that needs plenty of brushing to keep it silky smooth. Their sparkly eyes brighten any room, but it won't be long before these kittens are up to mischief!

 SHHH, TOP SECRET!

I'm a chatty cat. When I see you and meow I'm saying "Hi"!

 # BENGAL

KITTY PROFILE

Medium to large

Black and browns with patterns

Any

★★★★

Small wild cats and Bengal pussycats share a special beauty. Their coats are patterned with spots, stripes, marbling, or rings of color called rosettes. Kittens are often extra fluffy, but as they grow bigger their thick fur will turn into the softest coat you will ever stroke.

SHHH, TOP SECRET!

Dogs like a bath, but I prefer a shower– I love water!

BICOLOR SHORTHAIR

KITTY PROFILE

🐾🐾🐾 Medium to large

Two colors such as black/white or tabby/white

👁👁 Any

🐈 ★★

Black and white shorthair cats are much-loved in homes all over the world. They are playful and smart, but they also like to be left alone. Even these cuddly kittens enjoy their own space, and time to just sit and watch the world go by.

SHHH, TOP SECRET!

I'm easygoing, but if you ignore me I'll come over and bump you with my head!

 # BIRMAN

KITTY PROFILE

 Medium

Ivory, fawn, cream

Blue

★★★★

When a Birman kitten is born it has big round eyes and it is white all over. As it gets older, the kitten's fur changes color and becomes darker on the legs, face, tail, and ear tips. Its feet, however, stay white forever...unless it runs through muddy puddles!

SHHH, TOP SECRET!

I'm a quiet cat with a soft mew. I chirrup when I see someone I like!

 # BOMBAY

KITTY PROFILE

 Medium

Black

Copper, gold, yellow-green

★★★

When a jet-black Bombay kitten stirs from its sleep, it's ready for action—these cats are busy, playful, and loving. If a Bombay doesn't get enough attention, it might tap you on the arm or bump you with its head to remind you that it needs cuddles.

SHHH, TOP SECRET!

If you throw scrunched-up balls of paper, I'll run and fetch them for you!

BRITISH BLUE SHORTHAIR

KITTY PROFILE

 Medium to large

 Blue

 Copper, orange

 ★★

Children make perfect playmates for these big-hearted cats, which are easy-going and have plenty of patience. Even the kittens are as soft and gentle as a tiny teddy bear! British Shorthair cats are heavy and strong, and they take five years to reach their full size.

SHHH, TOP SECRET!

If you pick me up I'll wriggle out of your arms—I don't like being carried!

BRITISH WHITE SHORTHAIR

KITTY PROFILE

 Medium to large

 White

 Copper, orange, blue

 ★★

These adorable kittens look like furry angels, but they are as naughty as pixies! They will grow up to become quiet, gentle, and friendly cats who spend lots of time grooming their fur. They will use their rough tongues to lick away any signs of dirt on that lovely white coat.

SHHH, TOP SECRET!

Some white shorthairs have one blue eye and one copper eye!

 # BURMESE

KITTY PROFILE

 Small to medium

Blue, brown, chocolate, cream, lilac, red

Yellow, gold

★★★

Beautiful Burmese kitties are practically perfect in every way. They are smart, funny, playful, and they have soft, silky fur. They love to be brushed, and their purr is almost as loud as their meow! A Burmese is a best friend forever.

SHHH, TOP SECRET!

I love you to pieces, but I will cry and wail if you don't love me back!

28

 # BURMILLA

KITTY PROFILE

 Medium

 Silver-white with darker tips

 Yellow, gold, green

 ★★

Cats are curious creatures, and these little kittens love to investigate the insides of cupboards and under beds. Burmilla cats can have long hair, or short hair, but they are always pale in color. They make friendly, loving pets that prefer peace and quiet.

 SHHH, TOP SECRET!

Kittens often have tabby stripes on their tails or legs, but they usually disappear.

 # CHARTREUX

KITTY PROFILE

- Medium to large
- Blue with a silvery sheen
- Yellow, gold, orange
- ★★

Their woolly blue fur will keep these kittens warm outside, even when it's snowing. Chartreux cats love to hunt, so they enjoy living with families who have time to play catching games with them. They need to be brushed every week, especially in warm weather.

SHHH, TOP SECRET!

If you call my name I'll come running to greet you with a head rub!

CORNISH REX

KITTY PROFILE

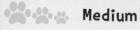 Medium

 Any

 Gold, blue, green, hazel

 ★★★★

Those huge ears don't only make a Cornish Rex kitten look good, they help it to hear quiet sounds, too. These kitties have very short, wavy fur so they feel the cold and prefer to stay inside or lie in the sun. Cornish Rex cats are friendly, funny, and playful.

SHHH, TOP SECRET!

In the winter I need a coat and in the summer I might need sunscreen!

34

EGYPTIAN MAU

KITTY PROFILE

 Medium

Silver, bronze, smoke, black

Gooseberry green

★★★★

Cheetahs, jaguars, and leopards are spotted wild cats, but have you ever seen a spotted pet cat before? When an Egyptian Mau is feeling especially happy, it does a strange waggle walk. It marches with its back in one spot while wiggling its tail!

SHHH, TOP SECRET!

I am super-speedy. I can run faster than nearly all other cats!

GINGER SHORTHAIR

KITTY PROFILE

 Medium to large

 Red

 Copper, gold, green-yellow

 ★★★

The stunning ginger color of these cats can occur in almost any type of cat, especially British Shorthair and Longhairs. There are tabby stripes and spots, as well as a dark "M" shape above the eyes. Ginger cats and kittens are famous for their lovely faces and friendliness.

SHHH, TOP SECRET!

My fur color is called "red" or "ginger" but I think it's gorgeously golden!

HAVANA BROWN

KITTY PROFILE

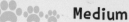 Medium

 Deep brown

Green

★ ★ ★

The lean body, long legs, and long face of these chocolate brown kitties tell you that they are related to Siamese cats. They are just as delightful and chatty as a Siamese, too. Havana cats are very curious and often disappear into drawers, cupboards, and cardboard boxes!

SHHH, TOP SECRET!

I love company and I hate to be left alone. It makes me sad.

KORAT

KITTY PROFILE

 Medium

 Blue-gray with silver tips

 Green

★★★

The Korat cat comes from a hot country called Thailand, where it is thought to bring good luck. A cute Korat kitten was a popular gift for Thai people getting married! Now Korats are loved all over the world, especially by children, who like their sassy nature.

SHHH, TOP SECRET!

Some kittens are born with blue or amber eyes that turn green as they get older.

 # LaPERM

KITTY PROFILE

🐾🐾🐾 Small to medium

■■■ Any

👁👁 Any

🐈 ★★★

When a litter of LaPerm cats is born they usually have some curly hair, but it often falls out! Bald kittens feel the cold, but soon a new thick, curly coat grows and they are ready for action outdoors. Their ringlets and neck ruffs make these kittens especially adorable.

SHHH, TOP SECRET!

Even my whiskers and eyebrows are curly!

 # MAINE COON

KITTY PROFILE

 Large

Usually copper-brown with some black

Green, copper, gold

★★★★

A thick ruff of fluffy fur around a Maine Coon's neck and chest keeps it warm, even on the coldest days. These beauties are explorers, not lap cats, so snow and rain won't stop them from spending an afternoon outdoors. They can be skillful hunters.

SHHH, TOP SECRET!

When I am happy to see you I'll say "hello" with a soft chirp!

MANX

KITTY PROFILE

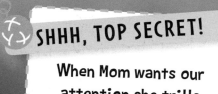

Medium

Any color or pattern

Any

★★★

Manx kittens are born with short tails, long tails, or no tail at all. They first came from the Isle of Man, near England, but now they live in many countries. Manx cats are strong, powerful cats that are famous for being able to jump very high.

SHHH, TOP SECRET!

When Mom wants our attention she trills at us. We always listen to Mom!

NORWEGIAN FOREST

KITTY PROFILE

 Large

Any color or pattern

Any

★★★

A thick coat of fur is very helpful when you live in the chilly northern country of Norway! The fur of a Norwegian Forest cat, also known as a Wegie, is thick and dries quickly. Kittens are fast learners and practice hunting almost as soon as they can run.

SHHH, TOP SECRET!

One of my favorite hobbies is to watch fish in a pond. I might even try to catch one!

 # OCICAT

KITTY PROFILE

 Medium to large

Various colors but with darker spots

Any except blue

★★

When an Ocicat comes indoors after an afternoon spent chasing bugs and climbing trees, you can expect it to greet you with a loud meow! It will need lots of cuddles to be reminded how much you love it—and who could say no to cuddling such a beautiful cat?

 **SHHH, TOP SECRET!**

I am an active cat that loves to run, chase, and climb everything.

PERSIAN BLUE LONGHAIR

KITTY PROFILE

🐾🐾🐾 Medium

⬛⬛⬜ Blue

👁👁 Copper

★★★

Like other Persians, these adorable kittens often snore! So if you can't find your kitten, you just have to look in warm, dark places and listen for the gentle rumble of a snoring baby. Persians have short, wide faces and heavy bodies. Their legs are quite short.

SHHH, TOP SECRET!

Cats have five toes on each of their front paws, but only four toes on each back paw.

PERSIAN WHITE LONGHAIR

KITTY PROFILE

 Medium

 White

 Blue, copper, gold

 ★★★

Although most cats like to spend time outdoors, Persians are happy to stay at home and sleep on your lap. Even kittens find life indoors is exciting enough! These cats have very long, fluffy fur, so they need to be brushed every day to keep them clean and neat.

SHHH, TOP SECRET!

I'm a big fan of doing as little as possible!

56

# RAGAMUFFIN

KITTY PROFILE

🐾🐾🐾 Medium to large

◼◼◼◻ Any

👁👁 Any

🐱 ★★

As soon as a Ragamuffin kitten opens its eyes, it's ready for action. It enjoys scampering around the house, but its favorite hobby is being picked up, stroked, hugged, and kissed! These are some of the sweetest, quietest, and most lovable cats around.

SHHH, TOP SECRET!

If you look between my toes you'll see a tuft of fur poking out!

58

# RAGDOLL

KITTY PROFILE

- 🐾🐾 Large
- Pale with some dark patches
- 👁👁 Blue
- ⭐⭐

When a Ragdoll kitten looks at you with its big blue eyes, your heart will melt. Ragdolls are real softies with long, silky fur. This cat loves to be cuddled so much it will flop into your arms and purr as soon as you pick it up. It will be fast asleep in minutes!

SHHH, TOP SECRET!

When you cuddle me my body goes floppy, like a ragdoll!

RUSSIAN BLUE

KITTY PROFILE

 Medium

 Blue with silver tips

 Emerald green

★★

A Russian Blue is like a silver ghost-cat that disappears when there are strangers around! Even the kittens are easily scared and shy, but that doesn't stop them from cuddling up with the family and playing fetch. These cats can even be trained to walk on a leash.

SHHH, TOP SECRET!

If you stroke me you will discover my blue coat is thick and plush, like velvet.

 # SAVANNAH

KITTY PROFILE

 Large

Black, browns with patterns

Yellow, gold, brown

★★★★★

Most cats enjoy spending hours fast asleep in warm places, but a Savannah cat has no time for idleness. These playful pets are far too busy to sit around when there are things to chew, climb, or creep up on. Savannahs are wild, wonderful, and hard work!

SHHH, TOP SECRET!

I'm the perfect cat for families who love dogs!

# SCOTTISH FOLD

KITTY PROFILE

🐾🐾🐾🐾 Medium to large

■■□ Any

👁👁 Any

★★★★★

When a mother Scottish Fold cat gives birth to her litter of kittens they all have straight ears. Over the next few weeks the ears of some kittens begin to curl forward. They are known as Scottish Folds, while their straight-eared brothers and sisters are called Scottish Straights!

SHHH, TOP SECRET!

I have a round face and big eyes. Some people say I look like an owl!

SIAMESE

KITTY PROFILE

🐾🐾🐾 Medium

▪️▪️▪️◻️◻️ Pale body with darker face, legs, ears, and tail

👁👁 Blue

⭐⭐

With its slender body and short, silky fur, a Siamese cat feels the cold. So don't be surprised if one of these elegant kittens decides to climb up your body, wrap itself around your warm shoulders, and purrs loudly! Siamese cats wail rather than meow.

SHHH, TOP SECRET!

I don't like other cats, or people very much. But I do love you!

68

SINGAPURA

KITTY PROFILE

 Small to medium

Ivory-gold with dark bands and cream

Yellow, gold

★★★★

All cats are playful, but Singapuras are some of the sassiest, funniest, and most playful cats of them all. Some people say they stay kittens forever. A favorite trick of a Singapura is to climb somewhere high so it can watch everyone moving around below.

SHHH, TOP SECRET!

If I get cold I'll sneak into your bed and ask you to warm me up, quickly!

SNOWSHOE

KITTY PROFILE

 Medium to large

Pale body with a darker face, tail, and legs

Amber, green, or hazel

★★★★

Snowshoe cats have four white feet. A snowshoe's white front paws are called "mittens" and its white back paws are called "boots". These kittens are gorgeous, with sparkling eyes and a love of water. When they are older they may enjoy a warm bath.

SHHH, TOP SECRET!

Some people call me "Silver Laces" because of my silvery-white feet.

73

SOMALI

KITTY PROFILE

 Medium

Usually golden, golden-red, or golden-brown

Amber, green or hazel

★★★★

Kittens are not allowed outside, on their own, until they are about six months old. It's a long time to wait for energetic Somali kittens, who need lots of space. Somalis don't like being indoors when the sights and sounds of nature are calling them to come and play!

SHHH, TOP SECRET!

Some people call me a fox-cat because of my lovely color and furriness.

 SPHYNX

KITTY PROFILE

🐾🐾🐾 Medium

⬛⬛⬜ Any

👁👁 Any

🐈 ★★★★★

The elegant, playful Sphynx is a most unusual cat—it is hairless! Not all Sphynxes are completely bald—they have a very fine coat of fuzz instead. Kittens look peculiar because they have huge eyes and ears, and their skin is super-soft and wrinkly.

SHHH, TOP SECRET!

I look skinny, but I have a big appetite. I need lots of energy to keep warm!

TABBY LONGHAIR

KITTY PROFILE

 Medium to large

Silver, brown, black, ginger with some cream areas

Yellow, gold, green, hazel

★★★

A tabby cat is also called a tiger cat because it has dark stripes, and sometimes spots, on its thick coat of fur. Longhair tabbies can become huge balls of fluff if they are not brushed every day. It's lucky these sassy kittens love lots of attention!

SHHH, TOP SECRET!

Dark stripes above my eyes make the letter "M".

TABBY SHORTHAIR

KITTY PROFILE

Medium to large

Silver, brown, black, ginger with some cream areas

Yellow, gold, copper, green, hazel

★★★★

Tabby kittens are clever, cute, and playful, with lots of energy for exploring. Some tabbies even love to play fetch, just like a dog. Shorthair tabbies are adorable pets in the house, but they look like tiny tigers as they prowl around the garden.

SHHH, TOP SECRET!

We are loved all over the world because we are beautiful, bright, and bouncy!

TIFFANIE

KITTY PROFILE

Small to medium

Black, blue, chocolate, lilac, red, cream

Yellow, gold, green

★★★

A Tiffanie cat is the perfect pet for families who like strong, healthy cats with long hair and a playful nature. Just like human babies, these kittens can be wide-awake and playing one minute, then be fast asleep the next! Young animals grow when they are sleeping.

SHHH, TOP SECRET!

We can be noisy cats, like our Burmese cousins. We will cry if you ignore us!

 # TONKINESE

KITTY PROFILE

 Medium

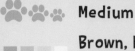 Brown, blue, chocolate, lilac, red, cream, apricot

 Blue, blue-green

★★★★

All kittens love the rough and tumble of family life. Playtime is the perfect time to explore, and learn how to hunt and climb, without getting hurt. Tonks, as these gorgeous cats are often called, stay kittenlike all their lives, so watch out for trouble!

SHHH, TOP SECRET!

I get very excited when someone rings the doorbell. I love everyone!

TORTIE LONGHAIR

KITTY PROFILE

Medium to large

A mixture of black, red, and cream or white

Yellow, gold, orange, green

★★★

The fur of a Tortie cat is the perfect patchwork of colors that make a beautiful pattern called "tortoiseshell". Many types of kittens can be born with Tortie colors, and some of them have tabby markings, too. Tortie Longhairs need to be brushed at least twice a week.

SHHH, TOP SECRET!

Tortie cats like us are often believed to bring good luck!

TORTIE SHORTHAIR

KITTY PROFILE

 Medium to large

A mixture of black, red, and cream or white

Yellow, gold, orange, green

★★★

When a Tortie cat is prowling through a garden, it can almost disappear. The mottled colors and long hair help it to hide in the dark shadows, so any birds or mice nearby need to watch out! Torties are known to be bold and curious cats.

SHHH, TOP SECRET!

Most tortoiseshell cats are females. Male torties are very rare.

TOYGER

KITTY PROFILE

 Medium to large

Dark stripes on brown or cream

Any color except blue

★★★★

Tigers have stripes and are the largest cats in the world. Toygers also have stripes, but luckily they are much sweeter than tigers. These tiny kittens are full of energy and fun. They will grow into active, sporty cats that even enjoy going for a swim on a warm day.

SHHH, TOP SECRET!

We love people, but we are not friendly to other cats, or dogs.

 # TURKISH ANGORA

KITTY PROFILE

 Medium

■■■□□ Any

Any

★★★★

These cute kittens need lots of attention from their mother who licks their long fur with her rough tongue to keep them clean. Like other bright cats, Turkish Angoras get bored quickly, so they are always delighted to meet new people who are willing to play with them.

SHHH, TOP SECRET!

If you brush or comb my silky hair every week, I will love you forever!

TURKISH VAN

KITTY PROFILE

Large

Mostly white with some color on head and tail

Amber or blue

★★

Not many cats like water, but Turkish vans don't just like it—they love it! These large cats are good swimmers, but curious kittens need to be kept away from water until they are strong enough to climb out of it by themselves.

SHHH, TOP SECRET!

If you hear a sudden splash, it might be me going for a swim!